EXPLORING DEVON & CORNWALL'S BRANCH LINES

John Jackson

AMBERLEY

First published 2020

Amberley Publishing
The Hill, Stroud
Gloucestershire, GL5 4EP

www.amberley-books.com

ISBN 978 1 3981 0239 2 (print)
ISBN 978 1 3981 0240 8 (ebook)

British Library Cataloguing in Publication Data.
A catalogue record for this book is available from
the British Library.

Typesetting by Aura Technology and Software
Services, India. Printed in the UK.

Contents

Introduction

I remember the day I took my first train ride across the county boundary into Devon. It was on a family holiday in the summer of 1963. We were staying at Weston-super-Mare and, no doubt in return for a commitment to good behaviour, I had been promised a train ride along the sea wall at Dawlish. My love affair with the West Country had begun. I do remember passing Dawlish's sea wall that day, but little else in my memory from that holiday remains, other than that we had seen the Cliff Richard movie *Summer Holiday* in a local cinema the previous day.

Our exploration of the branch lines of Devon and Cornwall begins in that same decade, the 1960s. Unbeknown to this youngster at the time, our railways were under increasing scrutiny with their huge financial losses under the political spotlight. So, let's turn the clock back fifty years or so and set the rail scene of the day.

Half a century ago our railways went through the biggest rationalisation in their 200-year history. The need to drastically cut running costs became a priority for the government of the time. The entire rail network was put under close scrutiny as a plan to remodel the country's rail map was developed.

The map of passenger railway lines had already seen some pruning since nationalisation after the Second World War. What happened next was far more drastic. The infamous 'Beeching Axe' fell on around 33 per cent of the nation's passenger railway lines, as the resultant recommendations of Dr Richard Beeching were adopted by the parliament of the day.

Although some of the country's main lines were included in these proposals, it was inevitably Britain's branch lines that were in the firing line. Widespread closures in the 1960s virtually brought an end to the romantic notion of a one or two coach loco-hauled train trundling a few miles from a main-line junction to a small-town destination 'in the middle of nowhere'.

Some branch lines did survive and, historians would say, it was a bit of a lottery as to which ones did so. Political influences undoubtedly played a part. The Beeching Axe was to fall more heavily in some areas, particularly, and more understandably, where the local population was much more sparsely spread.

Take a look at a railway map prior to these cuts and it shows that the West Country counties of Devon and Cornwall suffered alongside the rest of the UK.

Sizeable towns, and the smaller wayside stations along the route, were wiped from the railway landscape. Younger readers may be surprised to learn that it was not just the Great Western Railway (GWR) that served the people of these two counties. The Southern Railway ventured deep into what is now regarded as GWR territory, although the traveller has to look hard to find any traces of that today.

That company's flagship service was the 'Atlantic Coast Express', which offered an alternative service from London to the West Country, with through carriages offered to a variety of destinations until the mid-1960s. These included Ilfracombe, Padstow and Bude; just some of the sizeable communities that we were to lose their rail services completely under the wide-sweeping cuts outlined above.

The cuts happened at a time when this particular schoolboy was just becoming old enough to enjoy such train rides to the seaside! In an earlier title for Amberley Publishing, *Survivors of Beeching*, I looked at the national picture of some of those lines that escaped closure. In this publication, it is the survivors in Devon and Cornwall that are worthy of a much closer look.

A number of secondary lines in Devon and Cornwall did, thankfully, survive and their future looks as secure today as it has ever been. This book, then, is a twenty-first-century exploration of the lines of Devon and Cornwall.

Our journey commences in the Devonshire city of Exeter. It remains an important railway interchange for travellers heading across the county. The city itself, perhaps remarkably, still boasts three stations bearing the name 'Exeter' and a fourth serving St James' Park. Our journey's end will be at the extreme western end of the Great Western Main Line (GWML) at the Cornish terminus of Penzance.

The journey between Exeter and Penzance along the GWML covers a total of just over 130 miles, with a number of branch lines diverging at calling points along its route. Most of these continue to enjoy passenger services, with a few others surviving to serve the limited amount of freight traffic still to be found in the West Country.

The area's numerous mines were a feature of the industrial landscape of the area dating back to the Industrial Revolution. Almost all of these have long since disappeared. The county of Cornwall was once a source of employment for locals working in the lead, tin and china clay industries. Today, just a reduced china clay operation remains with the traffic being handled by DB Cargo's small outbase at St Blazey, close to St Austell.

The West Country gateway of Exeter is well served by several passenger operators bringing passengers from many parts of the UK. Both Great Western Railway (GWR) and South Western Railway (SWR) offer services to and from London. GWR services operate from London's Paddington station, with SWR offering an alternative to and from London's Waterloo station. GWR also offer a service to Taunton, Bristol and Cardiff. CrossCountry complete the picture with longer distance links to Birmingham, north-west England, north-east England and Scotland.

GWR are owned by First Group. This company has operated the majority of the services in the West Country for twenty years or so. They repackaged their service under the GWR branding back in the Autumn of 2015, under a franchise agreement running until 2020 at the time of writing.

CrossCountry Trains is another long-standing brand owned and operated by Arriva. Their franchise agreement is also scheduled for renewal negotiations in late 2020.

So, in this book, we begin our journey in Exeter, heading broadly westwards to conclude at the Cornish outpost of Penzance. Our exploration of the 300 or so miles of Devon and Cornwall's railways not only explores this main artery but takes a look at the many branch lines along the way, namely:

Exeter to Barnstaple

The Exeter to Barnstaple Line is the only branch-line survivor that links the south and north of Devon, running for almost 40 miles north-westwards from Exeter. The railway is currently marketed as the 'Tarka Line', the name recognising the otter in Henry Williamson's book, which is set in the area.

The line gently meanders along a route that broadly follows the courses of the Yeo and Taw rivers, taking around an hour and a quarter to reach the North Devon terminus at Barnstaple.

Exeter to Exmouth

This 11-mile branch line between Exeter St David's and Exmouth hugs the River Exe until it reaches the river's estuary mouth. This branch line has been marketed as the 'Avocet Line' for a number of years, taking its name from the popular bird that frequents the river here.

Exeter to Paignton

This 30-mile line extends westwards along the South Devon coast before heading inland to the junction at Newton Abbot, and thence down the Torbay peninsula as far as Torquay and Paignton. This 'Riviera Line' skirts the sea wall between Dawlish and Teignmouth – one of the most photographed stretches of Britain's railways today.

Plymouth to Gunnislake

This 14-mile branch line leaves the GWML at St Budeaux and broadly follows the River Tamar on its forty-five-minute journey to its terminus at Gunnislake, just inside the Cornwall county boundary. Not surprisingly, the line has been branded the 'Tamar Valley Line'.

Liskeard to Looe

The 'Looe Valley Line' runs for 8 miles from the main-line junction at Liskeard to the seaside resort of Looe, with its compact station nestling on the bank of the river estuary of the same name.

Par to Newquay

The small community at Par provides the main-line junction for the 'Atlantic Coast Line', which runs just under 20 miles to the North Cornwall terminus at Newquay. A stretch of this branch line is also used for much of the rail-based china clay traffic that survives in Cornwall.

Truro to Falmouth Docks

This busy branch line leaves the GWML at Truro and heads 11 miles southwards to the town of Falmouth. The town's connections with the sea has earned the branch the title of the 'Maritime Line'.

St Erth to St Ives

Just 4 miles long, the final Cornish branch line runs from the junction at St Erth to the popular tourist centre of St Ives. Travel along the 'St Ives Bay Line', which offers panoramic views of the bay from which the line takes its name.

All the above lines remain part of the National Rail UK network. The two counties are also home to a number of preserved and heritage railways in the hands of private operators, chiefly run by enthusiasts and volunteers. These latter lines are mentioned during our journey. Space, however, precludes the more detailed look that each deserves.

We'll also take a look at what freight traffic remains to the west of Exeter. I have chosen to concentrate them in a section of their own. The content that follows reflects my understanding of the two counties' railways as at the end of 2019.

Finally, I hope that you, the reader, enjoy your journey through these pages as much as I have enjoyed compiling them.

John Jackson

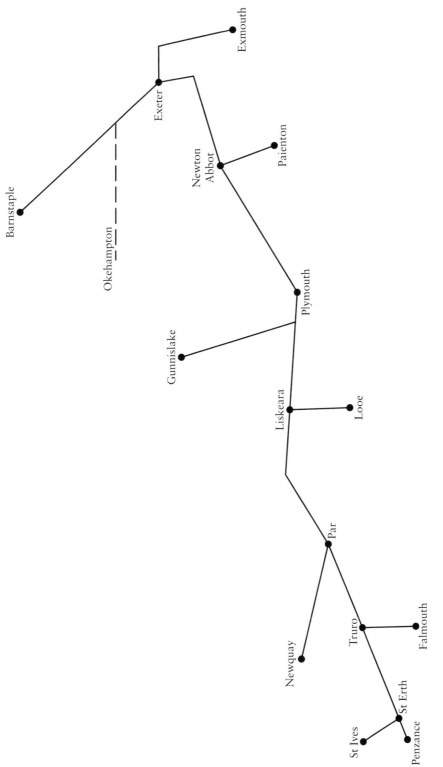

West Country Lines 2015

Barnstaple

Exmouth

Exeter

Okehampton

Newton
Abbot

Paienton

Plymouth

Gunnislake

Liskeara

Looe

Par

Newquay

Truro

Falmouth

St Erth

St Ives

Penzance

My sketch map of the rail lines in Devon and Cornwall, drawn *c.* 2015.

Exeter

Our journey begins at one of Exeter's two main stations, St David's. The other, Exeter Central, is included in the Exeter to Exmouth section of this book. High Speed Train (HST) sets have been the mainstay of London services for around forty years, operating between Penzance, Plymouth, Exeter St David's and London's Paddington station. On 1 June 2016, power car No. 43190 is seen waiting on the rear of a Paddington-bound service.

Around fifty services a day operate on this Paddington route, the majority of these taking the direct route between Taunton and Reading, a journey of just over 150 miles. On 11 May 2019, No. 43198 *Oxfordshire 2007* stands at St David's. This power car carries the revised livery of the operator's latest Great Western Railway (GWR) branding.

South Western Railway offer an alternative service between Exeter and London's Waterloo station, operated by Class 158 and 159 diesel units. These trains leave the opposite end of St David's station curving sharply eastwards towards Central station. On 1 June 2013, No. 159106 forms a three-coach service to Waterloo.

The long-distance services to and from Birmingham and beyond are operated by CrossCountry Trains using their fleet of Voyager diesel units. On 11 May 2019, No. 220031 is seen passing Red Cow Crossing, immediately to the north of St David's station.

The fleet of diesel units for local services in the West Country is often stretched. A part solution was the daytime use of the loco from the overnight sleeper working with a short rake of coaching stock. On 28 May 2016, No. 57605 *Totnes Castle* has just terminated at Exeter St David's on one such service.

Many of the local fleet of diesel units are serviced at Exeter Traincare Depot, adjacent to St David's station. On 24 May 2015, the depot is home to unit Nos 143621, 150124 and 153382.

In this view taken on 11 May 2019, unit No. 158763 stands at the depot's buffer stops. Since this photo was taken, work has commenced on additional depot accommodation, including a new car wash, a three-track maintenance shed and offices.

On 28 May 2016, units No. 150247 and No. 153325 are seen leaving St David's on a service to Barnstaple. The train will leave the main line at Cowley Bridge Junction, around 1 mile north of here.

Exeter to Barnstaple (Tarka Line)

The first station on the branch line to Barnstaple is at Newton St Cyres, just over 4 miles out of Exeter. The isolated station has a single platform but very few services call here, even on request. On 1 December 2019, No. 150232 passes through on a morning service to Barnstaple.

The next station is Crediton, where both platforms have been retained and services are scheduled to pass here. This photo shows the view from the footbridge, built in 1878 and virtually unchanged since, looking towards Exeter. The station buildings on the left include a privately run tearoom.

The signal box remains open at Crediton and controls most of the branch, albeit with a No Signalman Token Remote (NSTR) system. The driver of an Exeter-bound four-coach service, with unit No. 150234 leading, pauses at the box to exchange the token with the signalman.

The token retrieved by the signalman will shortly be handed to the driver of the next northbound unit, No. 150219. It is seen here pausing at the platform on a morning service to Barnstaple.

There is a well-cared-for appearance to the station at Crediton, reflecting the hard work of the Friends of Crediton Station. In addition, a number of items of railwayana are still in evidence. These include the bridge crossing notice of the L&SWR (London & South Western Railway), which became part of the Southern Railway in 1928.

A distance of 10 miles from Exeter and the line reaches the single platform station at Yeoford. This platform was once the southbound platform, but now Exeter to Barnstaple trains in both directions use it. The line to the right passes the disused northbound platform. This line is, in fact, now operated as a separate single-line branch from Crediton to Okehampton, covered later in this publication.

The next station is Copplestone and from here the railway line and the A377 will run side by side all the way to Barnstaple. Unit No. 150232 slows to call here on request on a service from Barnstaple to Exeter.

15 miles from Exeter and the wayside station at Morchard Road is reached. This single-platform station takes its name from the village of Morchard Bishop around 3 miles away.

2 miles further and the line reaches Lapford with a single platform surviving to serve the handful of passengers that use this wayside halt each day.

We've now reached the halfway point on the line from Exeter to Barnstaple, and the two-platform station at Eggesford. It bustles in comparison to other village halts, but only when the hourly train services meet using the passing loop here. The tokens for the sections to Crediton and to Barnstaple are exchanged here. A four-coach service, with No. 143617 leading, pulls into the loop on a Barnstaple-bound working.

Meanwhile, a single Class 150 unit, No. 150219, arrives at the southbound platform on a service to Exeter. The driver will shortly collect the token for the section to Crediton.

The signage at Eggesford station has been updated to include both the Tarka Line branding and the GWR logo and colours. Once, the station was a private one for the benefit of the Earl of Portsmouth. Today, it serves as the nearest rail point for the nearby town of Chulmleigh.

Having passed through the rural station at Kings Nympton, the Earl's stamp on this area is borne out by the little station at Portsmouth Arms, the name of a nearby hostelry. There's little evidence of the signal box that once stood on the platform here, with the station offering the minimum of facilities.

On an isolated piece of track adjacent to Portsmouth Arms station stands this Pullman car, named *Aries*. Dating back to 1952, it was the last Pullman car to be built at the company's workshops at Preston Park, near Brighton.

The station at Umberleigh is just 6 miles from Barnstaple. The Southern Railway colours on the vintage platform sign are a reminder of the line's past.

On 2 December 2019, unit No. 150248 leads a four-coach service into the single platform at Umberleigh. The train is heading towards Exeter.

A little over a mile and half from Umberleigh, the branch line serves the last intermediate station, Chapelton. The former station house here is now a private residence, standing alongside the disused southbound platform.

The single platform is now used by only a small number of trains calling, with most passing without stopping, even on request. The passenger numbers at this, one of the least used stations in the UK, can be measured in hundreds rather than thousands annually. This is the view looking towards Barnstaple with the former station house on the right.

Today's journey's end on the branch line is at Barnstaple. The station here was known as Barnstaple Junction until the 1970s. This reflected the number of travel options then available in the area, with lines to Torrington, Bideford, Taunton and Ilfracombe. The impressive station building here remains and gives a hint of those bygone days.

Barnstaple station retains a manned ticket office, and the whole room still reflects its past history with the familiar SR green livery in evidence. London Waterloo is 210 miles from here via Exeter.

Today, Barnstaple is served by fourteen trains each weekday, providing a broadly hourly service to Exeter, with most trains continuing to Exmouth. Unit No. 143618 stands in platform 1 waiting to leave on one such service. The use of more modern, air-conditioned Class 158 units on the branch is a future promise.

Work is underway here to reopen platform 2 on the right, to improve operational flexibility on the 40-mile line. The line – beyond the buffer stops and behind the camera – used to run through to Ilfracombe. This trackbed now forms the Tarka Trail for walkers and cyclists to enjoy the estuary of the rivers Taw and Torridge.

Crediton to Okehampton

This stretch of Devon's branch lines is chiefly in the hands of the Dartmoor Railway. I have included a mention here because the line also sees a service, limited to summer Sundays, operated by GWR through to Exeter. The well-maintained station at Okehampton is seen in this view looking towards Crediton.

The preserved signal box at Okehampton is housed at the end of platform 1. In this view, the line beyond continues to Meldon Quarry, once used to provide ballast for the rail industry, but the line was sold to private enterprise as part of rail privatisation in the 1990s.

The coaching stock of the Dartmoor Railway can be seen in this Okehampton view, taken from the station footbridge. The former goods shed on the right is now converted as a youth hostel for Okehampton.

The former BR diesel shunter numbered 08937 is at the head of this rake of coaching stock. It now carries its previous number, D4167.

The station at Sampford Courtenay, between Okehampton and Crediton, is served by the GWR service often referred to as the 'Sunday Rover'. With no facilities on the platform, the gate is opened just before scheduled train departures. At Okehampton, a connecting bus service operates to Gunnislake to enable a 'round robin' journey back from there to Exeter.

In the opposite direction from Okehampton is Meldon. The quarry here is now disused and the current operational line stops short of the nearby Meldon viaduct, the start of which is seen on the left in this photo.

Exeter to Exmouth (Avocet Line)

This 11-mile branch line from St David's to Exmouth takes a sharp curve immediately after leaving St David's in order to reach Exeter Central. On 15 July 2015, No. 150124 is seen approaching St David's on the curve from Central station, on a service from Exmouth to Paignton.

Although Central station is much smaller than St David's, passenger usage runs at around 2.5 million a year, roughly the same as St David's. On 19 November 2015, two-car unit No. 150101 calls at Central on a service to Exmouth.

Central station is Exeter's most convenient station for many of the city's amenities. Formerly known as Queen Street when opened by the London & South Western Railway, it was rebuilt in the 1930s, and is now operated by GWR. This view of the station front was taken on 19 November 2015.

The South Western Railway-operated line to London Waterloo diverges at nearby Exmouth Junction, with local stations at St James' Park and Polsloe Bridge either side of this junction. In this shot, No. 150207 calls at the next station, Digby & Sowton. This park'n'ride station is 3 miles from St David's and also a short walk from Sandy Park, the home of Exeter Chiefs Rugby Club.

The station signage here incorporates the branding of First Great Western along with that of the Avocet Line. The popular bird is a regular visitor to the nearby Exe river estuary.

Having passed through Newcourt, trains heading both north and south are scheduled to pass at the next station, Topsham, the branch's halfway point. On 1 June 2016, No. 153370 enters the passing loop at Topsham on a service for Exmouth. The three-car train also has single-car units Nos 153382 and 153325 in its consist.

The signal box at Topsham was taken out of use in 1988. It is a Grade II listed building and has therefore survived, next to the busy level crossing here.

Just a mile and a half further and the quiet station at Exton is reached. This shot on 3 December 2019 shows the single-platform station looking towards Exeter.

The reason why Exton is my favourite station on the branch is evident in this shot. Turn the camera around 90 degrees from the previous photo and this is the view. Standing on this quiet, rural station there is a splendid view on offer over the Exe Estuary.

The restricted station at Lympstone Commando, for the Royal Marines base, is followed almost immediately by the station serving the village of the same name. Unit No. 150238, leading on a four-coach working, calls at Lympstone Village bound for Exmouth.

The branch terminus is at Exmouth, 11 miles from Exeter St David's. On 3 December 2019, unit No. 150243 approaches the single platform on a terminating service from Paignton.

A half-hourly service on the branch is maintained throughout the day, with trains running beyond Exeter to, alternatively, Paignton and Barnstaple. On 1 June 2013, No. 143603 has just terminated in the platform. The station once had four platforms with only the former platform 2 now remaining. The engine shed and signal box both closed in the 1960s.

Exeter to Newton Abbot & Paignton (Riviera Line)

Leaving Exeter St David's and heading west, the main line passes through the local Exeter station at St Thomas before reaching Starcross. On 3 December 2019, this view shows the station looking towards Exeter with No. 150238 leaving the platform. The Exe Estuary is on the right.

The Riviera Line hugs the bank of the Exe Estuary and the Devon coast for several miles. In this view, new unit No. 802109 heads for London Paddington on a service from Plymouth.

12 miles from Exeter the line reaches Dawlish Warren. Most CrossCountry Trains services run non-stop along this section. On 30 May 2013, four-car unit No. 220020 passes the station on a service to Paignton.

A few minutes later, an iconic HST set heads in the opposite direction on a service to London Paddington. The camping coaches on the left have been a familiar feature here for at least thirty years.

Another 1.5 miles along the coast and the railway reaches Dawlish. This is one of the most popular and most photographed stretches of railway in the UK. On 1 June 2013, power car No. 43128 leads a westbound HST along the sea wall through Dawlish station.

In common with many rail enthusiasts, the sea wall here has held my fascination since childhood. This view was taken in the summer of 1974 with a Class 47 and a Class 50 loco heading east on a summer Saturday service.

That summer of 1974 was the swansong for the 'Western' class on main-line passenger duties. Here an unidentified member of the class heads eastwards passing the bed and breakfast that was my home for the week!

The town of Teignmouth lies roughly halfway between Exeter and Paignton. It is described as the 'Gem of South Devon' on the station signage.

Most Paignton to Exeter stopping services through Teignmouth are extended to Exmouth. On 4 December 2019, a four-car working, with No. 143618 on the rear, calls on an Exmouth-bound service.

On the same day, No. 150221 leads No. 150238 as they approach the station on a working in the opposite direction.

20 miles from Exeter lies the junction station at Newton Abbot. The imposing station building here dates from 1927 and was designed by the then Chief Architect of the Great Western Railway, Percy Emerson Culverhouse.

Significant track rationalisation took place in the station area in the late 1980s. This has left a three-platform station to serve the main-line services from Exeter to Plymouth, as well as the Paignton branch. This photo was taken on 26 November 2017.

One of Newton Abbot's gantries with an impressive array of semaphore signals is now a prominent feature in the town centre.

On 26 November 2017, No. 150123, then still in First Great Western colours, waits in Newton Abbot's platform 1 to form the 1037 service to Paignton.

On 19 November 2015, all West of England to London services were still in the hands of HSTs. Power car No. 43017 is at the front of this service waiting to leave Newton Abbot station.

Power car No. 43171 leads this HST service arriving at Newton Abbot on 26 November 2017, a Sunday, on a service from Plymouth running to Bristol Temple Meads, rather than London Paddington. Services taking the Paignton branch veer off to the left in this picture.

Torre station is 3 miles from Newton Abbot and is a suburban station within the Torquay area. The tall signal box, although disused, remains intact as it is a Grade II listed building. This view is looking towards Newton Abbot.

GWR Class 158s now operate some of these branch services. On 3 December 2019, No. 158767 leaves Torre on a service to Paignton.

The main station in Torquay is close to the seafront. The station entrance is behind the camera in this photo with the Grand Hotel on the right. The proximity to Tor Bay is clearly evident.

The station is served by several CrossCountry Voyagers offering direct services to Birmingham and the North West. On 3 December 2019, No. 220031 calls on an early afternoon service to Manchester Piccadilly.

Services on the 28-mile line from Exeter reach journey's end at Paignton. The two-platform station here is the interchange between National Rail services and the preserved Dartmouth Steam Railway.

Paignton has, currently, three through trains a weekday to London Paddington. These are in the hands of GWR's fleet of Hitachi-built units. On 3 December 2019, No. 802101 waits to leave on the 14.54 service to London.

On the same day, No. 158767 leaves the station on a local service to Newton Abbot. The train is seen crossing the level crossing at the Torquay end of the platform, over the busy Torbay Road.

In this view the Network Rail station is on the left with No. 158767 in the platform. The Dartmouth Steam Railway is to the right with former Class 08 shunter, D3014 *Samson*, to the right. This preserved railway operates a service on the 7 miles to Kingswear.

Totnes & Plymouth

Heading westward from Newton Abbot, the GWML climbs Dainton Bank, the third steepest railway incline in the UK with a 2-mile stretch varying between 1 in 36 to 1 in 57, to reach the town of Totnes. On 4 December 2019, a pair of units, Nos 802011 and 802001, pass through Totnes station on a service to London Paddington.

On the same day, a CrossCountry HST calls at the station on a service to Plymouth. Power cars No. 43321 (nearer the camera) and No. 43378 are in charge of this service from Leeds.

Their HST counterparts operated by GWR are now confined to secondary services using shorter sets of coaching stock. Many of these iconic machines have been replaced by their modern Hitachi counterparts. In this view, Nos 43158 and 43155 are working 'back to back' from the depot at Laira, Plymouth to Wabtec at Doncaster.

The current signal box structure has stood on the station platform at Totnes for almost 100 years. It is a Grade II listed building and is now fulfilling a less familiar role as the station café.

Totnes was once the railway junction for the branch to Buckfastleigh and Ashburton. Today, services run from across the River Dart at Totnes Riverside station, operated by South Devon Railway.

This was the scene at the preserved South Devon Railway at Buckfastleigh in December 2019. Steam loco No. 3205 and Class 37 diesel loco No. 6737 are in the foreground.

A variety of locos are on view at the Buckfastleigh site, including Crompton Class 33 No. 33002 carrying its pre-TOPS number D6501 and named *Sea King*. The 7-mile branch from Totnes to Buckfastleigh once ran through to Ashburton. There is little evidence of the railway there today. The station site now houses a garage, with a pub close by appropriately called the Silent Whistle.

I couldn't leave commentary on Buckfastleigh without a glimpse of this bygone scene from the station platform. The milk churns remained part of the railway scene into the 1960s, and possibly beyond, evoking childhood memories of my first visits to the West Country.

On leaving Totnes, the GWML faces another challenge: climbing Rattery Bank. Whilst Dainton is the third steepest UK railway gradient, I am assured that Rattery ranks as the seventh. It is a 4-mile climb with a 1 in 45 gradient at its steepest. The recently reopened station at Ivybridge is passed before the line reaches the City of Plymouth. The depot at Laira is situated in a triangle of lines to the east of the city. In this view, one of the depot's resident diesel shunters, No. 08644, rests between duties.

The depot has a long association with the servicing of HST power cars and coaching stock, as well as, more recently, CrossCountry Voyagers. In this photo, GWR's No. 43170 stands alongside CrossCountry's No. 43357.

The lines around Plymouth were dealt a particularly severe blow under the Beeching closures of the 1960s. These included the lines to the left of this view of the depot, which included the track to the London & South Western Railway's station at Plymouth Friary, as well as branches within the harbour. The GWML to Plymouth's surviving station is on the right.

Today's station for Plymouth City Centre was rebuilt after the Second World War with eventual completion in 1962. This view shows the station building and entrance, which does not give a particularly inviting first impression on arriving here. It was formerly known as Plymouth North Road.

Many of CrossCountry's services terminate at Plymouth and, on 16 May 2019, four-car unit No. 220012 has just arrived on a service from the north of England.

GWR livery has been systematically applied to its fleet of rolling stock. Shortly after being so treated, No. 153373 waits at Plymouth on 30 May 2017 to form the 14.48 to Newton Abbot.

The same company has applied promotional colours to several of its units. Sister Class 153 unit, No. 153333, stands in one of Plymouth's bay platforms between duties. It is sporting vinyls inviting customers to 'visit South Devon'.

A range of promised improvements to services in the West Country is currently underway. A number of HST power cars are now formed with short sets of coaching stock on secondary services in the area. On 16 May 2019, No. 43186 with No. 43092 (nearer the camera) are seen heading west from Plymouth on a service to Penzance.

Plymouth to Gunnislake
(Tamar Valley Line)

As already mentioned, the Plymouth area saw drastic cuts in stations and services in the 1960s, with just one branch line surviving from Plymouth to Gunnislake. On 30 May 2017, No. 150120 arrives at Plymouth terminating on a Tamar Valley Line branch service.

These trains usually operate from Plymouth's west bay platform. On 16 May 2019, No. 150243 waits there whilst forming a service to Gunnislake.

While larger West Country towns such as Tavistock, Launceston and Callington lost their services, the first 14-mile journey on the Tamar Valley Line as far as Gunnislake was retained. Poor alternative road transport was cited as the reason for its last-minute reprieve. The Gunnislake branch leaves the main line at St Budeaux Junction and calls at Victoria Road station, seen here reflecting the Tamar Valley branding.

The single-track branch line soon passes the sidings at Ernesettle, as it skirts the bank of the Tamar River, with the bridge carrying the main line across the river towards Cornwall behind this photo. These sidings have seen infrequent use in connection with the MOD munitions and Royal Naval Armaments Depot here.

The next station is Bere Ferrers, 7 miles from Plymouth. The station sign here not only promotes the Tamar Belle Heritage Centre adjacent to the platform but is a Southern Railway reminder of the travel options once available to customers.

The Heritage Centre is home to a small collection of locos and coaches, including industrial shunter *A S Harris*, which has been stabled at Bere Ferrers for many years.

A further 3 miles along the branch is the station at Bere Alston, just 10 miles from the centre of Plymouth but it feels as if you've stepped back in time to another world. The redundant signal box remains intact on the disused station platform here. It was closed in 1970, two years after the line to Tavistock was axed. Since then the single-track line from Gunnislake to St Budeaux has been operated by token, ensuring only one train working on the branch.

On 30 May 2017, No. 150120 has just arrived on a service from Plymouth. The crew will now change ends as the unit heads towards Gunnislake. The line beyond to Tavistock and Okehampton was closed in 1966. Possible reopening, particularly to provide a diversionary route from Exeter to the west, remains under consideration. This debate gathers momentum whenever the sea wall at Dawlish is affected by extreme weather.

Credit is due to the local community for the upkeep of the branch-line stations. This is the view of the well-cared-for Bere Alston platform on 15 May 2019.

Shortly after leaving Bere Alston the viaduct at Calstock comes into view. The twelve-arch structure carries the railway across the River Tamar here.

Many of the branch line's rail passengers make the journey simply to enjoy the scenery on offer. There is no better view than the one on offer as the train passes over Calstock viaduct. Here, the train is slowing to call at the station, which is situated on the north bank of the river.

Today the end of the Tamar Valley line is at Gunnislake, 14 miles from Plymouth and just across the border from Devon into Cornwall. On 30 May 2016, No. 153373 stands in the single-platform terminus waiting to return to Plymouth.

The line beyond here used to run for a further 5 miles to the terminus at Callington. This stretch of line was also a victim of the 1966 closures. In the 1990s the station at Gunnislake was moved to its present site, enabling a low bridge to be demolished. On 27 May 2015, No. 150127 waits time to return to Plymouth.

Standing on the station platform enjoying the tranquillity, its hard to image that this area once had around 100 mines. The area was well known for its production of copper and tin. The station's welcome sign incorporates a reminder of Cornish Mining World Heritage status, as recognised by UNESCO.

Plymouth to Liskeard

On leaving Plymouth, the Great Western Main Line (GWML) soon reaches Brunel's famous Royal Albert Bridge, built in 1859, taking the line across the River Tamar and into Cornwall. This is the view of the bridge taken from Saltash, the first GWML station in Cornwall.

Almost immediately after crossing the bridge, the line continues across the Coombe viaduct in Saltash. This 2016 view of the viaduct is taken from the carriage window of a train crossing the Royal Albert Bridge.

St Germans station provides the passing customers with another reminder of days gone by. Next to the station are four former rail vehicles, now converted for holiday lets. This view shows former passenger luggage van No. 1353, which dates from 1896. It has been on this site since the mid-1990s.

Passing through the little-used station at Menheniot, the GWML reaches its next branch-line junction at Liskeard. On 11 May 2019, No. 802013 calls at Liskeard on a London Paddington service.

Two years earlier, on 28 May 2017, the previous order in the shape of HST power car No. 43002 *Sir Kenneth Grange* calls on the 12.33 to Paddington. By then this power car had become a celebrity. It had been outshopped in InterCity 125 livery and given its original cab end number, 253001.

On 14 May 2019, an unidentified Hitachi unit leaves Liskeard on an eastbound service. The Looe branch line veers to the left at the end of the platform, a surprise for some travellers as the town of Looe lies off to the right of this photo!

Liskeard to Looe (Looe Valley Line)

This delightful branch line survived the 1960s cuts, but only just. It came within a few weeks of closure before earning a last-minute reprieve. On 30 May 2013, No. 150219 stands in platform 3 at Liskeard on a Looe service. This platform is at right angles to the station's two main-line platforms.

The unit working the 9-mile-long Looe Valley Line on 28 May 2017 was single car No. 153361. It is seen here waiting at Liskeard to form the 12.47 service to Looe.

The line curves sharply on leaving the station and the Looe branch then passes under Liskeard viaduct, which carries the main line eastwards. This view of the viaduct on 30 May 2016 is taken from the branch-line train and the extent of the curve can clearly be seen.

On reaching Coombe Junction the unit reverses, the train staff being responsible for changing the points to enable the train to enter the section of line towards Looe.

Most passenger workings stop tantalisingly short of Coombe Junction Halt, as seen in this view from No. 150127 as it is in the process of reversing. The freight-only line continues past the station platform towards Moorswater. Incidentally, the word 'Halt' had been eliminated from railway station terminology until its inclusion here in 2008!

Just two workings a day serve this station in either direction. This is hardly surprising since it vies for the title of 'least used railway station' on an annual basis. The last ten years' figures show less than one passenger per day on average and I have not personally contributed to these figures since 2011! This is the afternoon service from Looe making a call in vain.

Curiously, the next station has also regained its 'Halt' status. St Keyne Wishing Well Halt enjoys a far superior service with around half of the services calling on request. The wishing well is located in the village of St Keyne, a few minutes' walk away.

The line continues through woodland passing the quaintly named stations at Sandplace and Causeland before following the estuary for the last 2 miles of its journey to Looe station. This is the unusual station sign made up of stones, viewed from the single platform with the river beyond.

Unusually, Looe station has always been formed of just a single track and platform and no run-round loop. Until the 1960s trains continued past the current stop point to a carriage and engine shed this side of the river bridge, in the background in this view.

This photo of No. 150265, standing at Looe on a return service to Liskeard, is taken from the buffer stops. It shows how little leeway there is to house a two-coach train in the platform.

Bodmin Parkway

The station, formerly Bodmin Road, was renamed in the 1980s. The station sign on the platform sums up the Cornish towns that were deprived of railway services in the mid-1960s, with bus transport the only option to reach this part of North Cornwall today. In addition, Parkway station itself is around 3 miles away from the town of Bodmin.

Platform three at Bodmin Parkway is used by the privately owned Bodmin & Wenford Railway. On 31 May 2017, the line had a special visitor in the form of steam loco No. 60163 *Tornado*.

They operate services from their headquarters at Bodmin General station. This view of the station exterior was taken on 12 May 2019.

These services operate from Bodmin General both towards Bodmin Parkway and Boscastle Junction. Steam loco No. 75178 is seen at the end of Boscastle Junction station about to run around its coaches for the return working.

In this view looking towards Bodmin General station, taken on 20 October 2011, former BR Class 08 shunter No. 08444 stands in the foreground. The former D3559 has been at the private railway for the last thirty years.

Today, there's little evidence of the railway's existence in this part of Cornwall. Wadebridge station is now home to the (John) Betjeman Centre, whilst Padstow station, seen here on 12 May 2019, is in use as the local council offices.

Lostwithiel & Par

The GWML continues westwards and, 6 miles from Bodmin Parkway, reaches Lostwithiel. On 15 May 2019, No. 150246 heads east from Lostwithiel, passing the Grade II former GWR signal box, on a service to Plymouth.

Most long-distance services between London Paddington and Cornwall pass here without stopping. On the same day, No. 802014 passes on a service to Penzance.

5 miles west of Lostwithiel, the GWML reaches the village of Par. On the evening of 31 May 2016, No. 57604 *Pendennis Castle* calls on the overnight sleeper service from Penzance to London Paddington.

Earlier that same day, power car No. 43026 leads a Paddington-bound service as it calls at Par. The days of these full-length GWR HST sets working through Par ceased during 2019. The platform to the right of the picture serves the Newquay branch.

Par to Newquay (Atlantic Coast Line)

Par's village station survived the 1960s railway cuts, chiefly as it sits at the junction of the branch line to Newquay, which also escaped the Beeching Axe. On 16 May 2016, No. 150247 leaves Par station and passes its signal box on a service to Newquay. Note the semaphore signals still in use here.

The local branch service is supplemented by a summer weekend CrossCountry working through to Newquay. The failure of the HST at Newquay on 29 May 2016 resulted in a lengthy delay. The return service was eventually operated by No. 57605 *Totnes Castle*, sent from Penzance, leading No. 43378 and its train. The service should have run through to Edinburgh but was eventually terminated at Plymouth.

The line heads north-westwards out of Par and soon passes alongside the freight yard at St Blazey. On 31 May 2016, No. 150128 has just passed the yard on a service to Newquay.

The station at Luxulyan is passed shortly after leaving St Blazey, before the line reaches the junction at Goonbarrow. Here, the signalman and driver exchange the token for the single-line section through to Newquay and back. This shot of the signal box was taken in 2012.

The Par to Newquay branch is around 20 miles long, with little or no population in between the junction and the terminus. What's more, the journey is one of around fifty minutes, unfavourable when compared with the main road that runs parallel. After passing the stations at Bugle and Roche, the train reaches St Columb Road. The station sign here reflects the 'Atlantic Coast Line' branding under which name the branch is marketed, reflecting Newquay's position on the Atlantic coast of North Cornwall. Patronage from this request stop runs at an average of around five passengers per day.

After leaving St Columb Road, the line passes through Quintrell Downs station before reaching its terminus at Newquay. On 28 May 2014, No. 150246 waits just a few minutes at the single-platform terminus before returning to Par.

Although an earlier train service has been pledged, this arrival from Par, worked by No. 150216 on 14 May 2019, reaches Newquay just after 10.00 and is the first arrival and departure of the day! This means passengers cannot arrive at Par, and connect with the rest of the rail network, before 11.00 daily. The alternative travel option, to Truro via Perranporth, was removed in the 1960s. Residents would, I am sure, prefer to travel to St Austell rather than Par but that, too, is not an option.

At Newquay, all the trackwork, signalling and signal box were removed during the 1980s and 1990s, leaving just a single track and platform with no loco run-round facilities. The nearby gasholder, a familiar local landmark, had also disappeared by then. The extensive goods yard had given way to a supermarket. On 30 May 2017, No. 150130 waits at the terminus to form the first train of the day to Par. Despite the restricted timetable, around 100,000 passengers use the station at Newquay each year.

Today's Freight Traffic in Devon and Cornwall

Let's pause on our westbound journey on the passenger lines in Cornwall and take a look at the surviving freight loco activity in the West Country. Sadly, it is possible to journey from Exeter through to Penzance and not see a single diesel loco. What traffic remains is centred on the area around Lostwithiel, Par and St Blazey. On 14 May 2019, No. 66126 sits outside the depot at St Blazey between duties.

The residual china clay traffic in Cornwall accounts for much of the remaining freight traffic in the area, and sees one, sometimes two, DB Cargo Class 66s based in the area. On 28 May 2015, No. 66078 approaches Par station with a typical working from Goonbarrow to Fowey.

The rail-borne china clay traffic had been chiefly operated on behalf of English China Clays plc (ECC) for most of the twentieth century. This company, in turn, was acquired in the 1990s by French-based Imery. Since the late 1980s, these trains have made use of a pool of wagons, designated as CDAs. On 2 June 2016, No. 375107 is seen in such a rake as it passes St Blazey Yard.

Imery's china clay is taken to Fowey Docks for export. Normally, on Mondays, Wednesdays and Fridays the traffic originates from Goonbarrow. On Tuesdays and Thursdays, it is despatched from Parkandillack. On the morning of 30 May 2017, a Tuesday, No. 66175 is seen passing Par station with a rake of empties bound for Parkandillack.

That same afternoon, No. 66175 is seen returning through Par station with a loaded working from Parkandillack to Fowey Dock Carne Point. In order to reach the Fowey Dock branch, these trains require a run around just to the east of Lostwithiel station.

A total of 124 CDA wagons were originally ordered by British Rail. Today, around a third of these have either been stored or have already been cut up. On 28 May 2015, some of these redundant wagons can be seen in St Blazey Yard.

On 20 October 2011, No. 66090 is seen passing through Lostwithiel station. It has just worked along the 4-mile-long branch from Fowey Dock and will now run around its rake of empties before heading westward to Goonbarrow, via Par.

Privately owned diesel shunters have been used to shunt wagons at both Goonbarrow and Parkandillack. On 30 May 2017, Imery's shunter No. P406D *Isaac* stands at Goonbarrow between duties.

On 2 June 2016, No. 66027 is seen approaching St Blazey with a loaded working from Goonbarrow to Fowey. The train will recess in St Blazey Yard.

This will enable the loco, No. 66027, to work a rake of JIA hoppers from St Blazey to Parkandillack. It is seen just an hour later waiting for the signal at Par so that it can pull forward to the loop beyond the station in order to run around and head west. It will then return to collect its original train from St Blazey and resume the diagram to Fowey.

The JIA wagons are also used on a long-standing working from St Blazey to Cliffe Vale, Stoke-on-Trent. In order to work over the Devon Banks, the consist is initially worked in two portions to Exeter Riverside, before onward movement north. On 28 May 2015, No. 66188 is seen passing Liskeard on its way to Exeter.

Around five hours later the Class 66 loco is seen passing through Par returning light engine to St Blazey.

On 15 May 2019, No. 66127 passes through Lostwithiel on a similar light engine working.

Adding a little variety to the freight traffic on offer, a sand flow has been operating in the last few years between Burngullow and Bow, in East London. On 14 May 2019, No. 66091 passes through Liskeard on the loaded London-bound working.

The autumn leaf fall period sees the use of a pair of DB Cargo Class 66 locos on a Rail Head Treatment Train (RHTT). With its base at St Blazey, these trains cover the main line and some West Country branches. On 26 November 2017, Nos 66027 and 66127 are in charge as the working approaches Newton Abbot station.

Two years earlier and on the same working, the locos in charge were Nos 66061 and 66067. They, too, are seen passing through Newton Abbot station.

Colas Rail operate into the West Country with a weekly, Wednesday-only flow from Aberthaw in South Wales to the Tarmac distribution centre at Moorswater in Cornwall. At the time this photo was taken, the train is scheduled to work through to Lostwithiel in order to run around before returning to Liskeard to gain access to the Looe branch. No. 70815 approaches Liskeard after that Lostwithiel run around on 31 May 2017.

The train then waits on the spur from the main line until the local Looe branch unit has cleared the road from Liskeard to Coombe Junction, to allow the Class 70 to proceed to the line's terminus at Moorswater. As at the end of December 2019, this resume covers all current freight activity in the West Country, with the exception of ad hoc ballast and engineering workings.

St Austell to Truro

Resuming our westbound journey from Par, the town of St Austell lies just 4 miles away. On 30 May 2013, power car No. 43188 leads an HST set into the platform. Today, the station offers convenient bus connections to the Eden Project, but little trace of its railway heritage remains.

I remember back in the 1970s the St Austell to Kensington Olympia Motorail service operating from here. There was also quite a large goods yard. All are now long gone. The signal box remains as a Grade II listed building, but was closed in 1980 when control for St Austell station area was transferred to the signal box at Par.

A further 15 miles to the south-west of St Austell, the GWML reaches Truro. The sixteen-arch Truro viaduct lies around 1 mile to the east of the city. Not only is it the longest viaduct in Cornwall, but it also offers a commanding view of the city with its cathedral dominating the cityscape.

On 29 May 2017, No. 60163 *Tornado* draws a huge crowd as it arrives at Truro on 'The Cornishman' from London to Penzance.

On 26 May 2015, power car No. 43187 passes the signal box and level crossing as it enters Truro station on a service from London Paddington to Penzance.

Less suitable for busy bank holiday services within Cornwall is the use of Class 150 units, as with a crowded No. 150216 arriving at Truro on 28 May 2014.

Truro to Falmouth (Maritime Line)

This 11-mile branch line is one of the busiest with a half-hourly service operating throughout the day. On 31 May 2016, a pair of Class 153 single-car units, with No. 153372 leading, wait to depart Truro for Falmouth Docks.

Trains taking the Falmouth branch diverge from the GWML towards Penzance at Penwithers Junction and it is a single-track line through to Falmouth Docks. A passing loop at Penryn was reinstated to allow this more intensive service to operate. The first station is at Perranwell, 4 miles from Truro. On 17 May 2019, No. 150244 passes on a service to Falmouth Docks.

The next station is Penryn, 8 miles from Truro. Here, the platform was extended, and the passing loop added around ten years ago. This has enabled a significant increase in the number of trains, now running at around thirty per day in each direction. In this view, units Nos 150247 and 150244 pass each other.

After passing Penmere station, which is now on the edge of Falmouth, the train arrives at Falmouth Town station itself. It offers access to the nearby National Maritime Museum which gives the line its name. Access is via a steep incline with extremely limited accessibility for the less able. No. 150247 is seen again on a branch service leaving Town station bound for Truro.

The line's terminus is at Falmouth Docks station. On 15 May 2015, No. 150239 is seen arriving on a service from Truro.

The station sign at Falmouth Docks invites passengers to alight for Pendennis Castle, which overlooks the Falmouth area. The castle has given its name to both a 'Castle' Class steam locomotive, No. 4079, presently undergoing work at Didcot Railway Centre and also Class 57 diesel loco, No. 57604, which still sees regular service on the London to Penzance sleeper trains.

Redruth to St Erth

The line beyond Truro passes through an area historically important for the mining industry with the town of Redruth at its heart. 7 miles from Truro, Redruth today offers a passenger connection, albeit by bus, to the town of Helston, once served by a railway branch line from the now closed junction station at Gwinear Road.

Passing through Camborne and Hayle, the line reaches its next branch-line junction at St Erth. On 29 May 2017, No. 150261 has just passed the signal box at St Erth and arrives at the westbound platform as it heads towards Penzance.

St Erth to St Ives (St Ives Bay Line)

The village station is also the busy junction for passengers travelling to St Ives. This is the scene on 31 May 2013 with passengers awaiting the arrival of the branch train in platform 3.

This platform can accommodate a four-coach train as seen here on 28 May 2014, with unit No. 150131 leading to St Ives. A half-hourly frequency is maintained throughout the day. During 2019, the park'n'ride facility which was previously at Lelant Saltings has also recently been relocated here.

The single-track branch may be only 4 miles long, but it skirts the bay and beach for much of its run. This is a typical scene from the carriage window looking down at the pristine sands.

Space is also tight at the terminus at St Ives. Since the early 1970s it has been reduced to a single platform in the area of the former goods shed. A footpath leads from the station to the nearby beach at Porthminster. Unit No. 150129 waits to depart leading a four-coach train to St Erth.

Penzance

Just 5 miles from St Erth, Penzance is the western terminus of the Great Western Main Line. The servicing depot at Long Rock is located on the edge of the town. On 20 October 2011, No. 57604 has removed the overnight sleeper from Penzance station to the depot for servicing. On this date, fuel was still delivered to the depot here by rail, as evidenced by the rake of tanks on the right.

This depot is usually home to a Class 08 diesel shunter. On 13 May 2019, No. 08410 is stabled at the head of a rake of stock when viewed from passing on the GWML.

Within Penzance station itself, little has changed since this view taken on 24 April 1983. Class 50 loco No. 50038 *Formidable* waits to leave platform 1 at the western terminus.

Over thirty years later, on 31 May 2016, and power cars Nos 43154 and 43023 are working an HST set in the same platform at the station. These HSTs on London services have gradually been replaced by five-car and nine-car Hitachi Class 802s since August 2018.

This view, taken on 29 May 2017, shows the station roof with Class 150 unit, No. 150002, standing in platform 3. The fourth platform is to the left of this shot, outside the enclosed roof area.

On 13 May 2019, power car No. 43156 waits in platform 4. It had arrived on a training run from Plymouth's Laira depot. These so-called short sets of HST stock were in the process of being introduced on secondary services, including those serving Devon and Cornwall.